JOHN
JOHNSON

Media Magnate

Keith Greenberg

ROURKE ENTERPRISES, INC.
VERO BEACH, FLORIDA 32964

A Blackbirch Graphics book.

Library of Congress Cataloging-in-Publication Data

Greenberg, Keith Elliot.
   John Johnson / by Keith E. Greenberg
     p. cm. — (Made in America)
   Includes index.
   Summary: Presents the life and accomplishments of the black entrepreneur who started "Ebony" magazine.
   ISBN 0-86592-033-8
   1. Johnson, John H. (John Harold), 1918– —Juvenile literature. 2. Publishers and publishing—United States—Biography—Juvenile literature. 3. Afro-American periodicals—Publishing—History—20th century—Juvenile literature. 4. Afro-American business enterprises—History—20th century—Juvenile literature. 5. Executives—United States—Biography—Juvenile literature. [Johnson, John H. (John Harold), 1918– . 2. Publishers and publishing. 3. Afro-Americans—Biography.] I. Title. II. Series.
Z473.J75G74 1993
070.5'092—dc20
  [B]   92-41751
                                        CIP
                                        AC

Contents

1

An Inspiration

"Failure is a word I refuse to accept."

In 1945, nobody would have ever expected a magazine about the positive aspects of African-American life to succeed. In several American states, blacks were treated very unfairly. They had to ride in the back of buses. They couldn't eat in the same restaurants as whites, and they weren't allowed to use the same bathrooms and drinking fountains as whites. A black athlete had yet to play in baseball's Major Leagues, and African Americans were separated into special units in the U.S. military.

Nevertheless, John H. Johnson started his magazine called *Ebony* anyway. With

Opposite: John Johnson challenged the practices of discrimination when he began publishing magazines specifically for African Americans.

lively photographs and interesting stories, the magazine would tell the story of black struggle, change, and achievements. Everyone from civil rights leader Martin Luther King, Jr. to entertainer Michael Jackson to basketball superstar Michael Jordan would find themselves written up in these pages.

"I've lived through all the changes," John said. Early in his life, people who looked down on black men, would call them "boy" in public. At that time, members of the race were referred to as "coloreds" and "negroes." Later, they'd be known as blacks, then Afro-Americans and, finally, African Americans. "We've come a long way," he reflected.

And *Ebony* has developed along with the culture. It has always stressed the strengths of African-American life. Many of the white owned magazines, on the other hand, have simply looked at such things as crime and drugs in the black community.

John's many other businesses would do more than just supply blacks with the same quality of products that whites possessed. His companies have been based on the understanding that African Americans—like every other ethnic group—are unique and need goods specially made for their tastes.

Role Model for Blacks

Today, John is seen as a role model for other blacks. During the 1940s, talented blacks were often advised to seek "lowly" jobs as maids or doormen. But John was willing to take a number of risks and become a publisher. "He was a generation ahead of everybody else," Alfred Edmond, of *Black Enterprise* magazine, said in 1990, "and he's been an inspiration to all black businesses in terms of what is possible."

Today, about 21 million people read John's magazines. Each month, 11 million people read *Ebony*, and 1.3 million read *EM* (the initials for his magazine *Ebony Man*). His popular *Jet* magazine draws 8.7 million readers every week.

The Johnson Publishing Company does much more than just publish magazines. It puts on the Ebony Fashion Fair, which is the world's largest traveling fashion show. It also produces beauty products and the Ebony Black Achievement Awards, a yearly celebration of African-American accomplishments in a variety of fields.

And John—who also owns radio stations in Chicago, Illinois, and Louisville, Kentucky—is listed as one of the richest men in America. He is so well admired that four presidents—Dwight D. Eisenhower, John F. Kennedy, Lyndon B. Johnson, and Richard M. Nixon—have appointed him to special commissions or ambassador's positions.

Constant Determination

To reach this level of achievement, John had to conquer not only racial discrimination, but poverty, too. As a teenager, his family was on welfare. He slowly rose to his present status by sticking to his motto: "Failure is a word I refuse to accept."

Linda Johnson Rice, John's daughter, is now president of Johnson Publishing. After her father retires, she will take over his position.

Forty years after *Ebony*'s first issue, one of the reporters for the magazine noted that the publisher still preferred hard work and long hours to enjoying life's luxuries. John arrived at the office before other employees, worked weekends, and took home reports to study at night.

John's employees have sometimes complained that he is a strict and demanding boss. They admit, however, that his attitude encourages them to push themselves harder. In John's own words, he sees his goal in the office as "teaching, training, leading, and demonstrating" for his workers.

Believing in Himself

As a young man starting out in the rough and uncertain world of business, John gained confidence from his mother's belief that he could do great things. As boss of a variety of businesses, he has tried to provide the same encouragement to his own family. Both his wife, Eunice, and daughter, Linda Johnson Rice, play major roles in Johnson Publishing. His daughter, in fact, is president of the company, and will someday inherit her father's position. And from the moment she was born, her father taught her to have faith in her ideas and values.

Living a Mother's Dreams

"She wanted me to be independent."

In almost every interview, John mentions his mother, Gertrude Johnson Williams. She was his greatest influence. He has described himself as "a person who wants to live up to the hopes that my mother had for me. My mother, who never went beyond the third grade, struggled and made all kinds of sacrifices because she wanted me to do better than she did. I'm very conscious of that."

John was born into poverty in 1918 in Arkansas City, Arkansas. John's father died when he was six years old, and his mother remarried. Her second husband quickly understood that Gertrude's first goal would always be striving for the success of her only child.

Early Training

While she was working as a cleaning woman, Gertrude encouraged her son to educate himself and to develop every skill. "She wanted me to be independent, so she taught me to cook, to wash clothes, to iron, to clean up behind myself," John recalled. "And to this very day, no one ever has to pick up my clothes or put my toothpaste back in the cabinet. These are things my mother taught me at an early age, and I have not moved away from them."

Despite her lack of formal schooling, Gertrude was a wise woman in her child's eyes. "She was one of the most educated people I've ever known," he said. "She was aware of the world. She wanted to see black people succeed. She was active in the church. She was a leader. Whatever group she ended up joining, she always became president. She was looked up to by people in the community....There was something about her that made her believe in herself and made her have great faith in education and, I guess, great faith in me."

John's mother was always his greatest source of inspiration. To help him succeed, she constantly encouraged her son to have faith in himself.

All this attention did not spoil John. His mother taught him that anything in his life was possible, but she stressed that no goals could be achieved without ambition and lots of hard work. "She taught me that you have to *earn* success, which means you have to prepare yourself, you have to work hard, you have to have commitment, and you have to have faith," he said.

Chicago—the Promise of a Better Life

In 1933, when John was 15, his mother decided to move to Chicago. Her husband didn't want to leave the warm climate of

Arkansas City and go north. But Gertrude insisted. She wanted her son to be an achiever, and she thought he'd be better off in a Chicago high school.

"The Arkansas of that period was not a good place to raise a son from whom she expected great things," John explained.

Gertrude arranged for her son to move in with a friend in Chicago. She worked as a cook for two years to save the money for the trip. While Gertrude and her husband looked for jobs, the boy attended Chicago's DuSable High School.

A Matter of Pride

There were no jobs for John's parents in Chicago. Unfortunately, the family was forced to go on welfare. This situation truly embarrassed John. He recalls sitting outside with a group of friends, watching a truck roll down the block, bringing food to families on welfare. When the truck arrived at his house, John told the others that he didn't live there. Then, when the truck went to one of the other teenager's houses, the boy also claimed to live somewhere else. "We all knew the trucks were going to our houses," John said, "but we were just too ashamed to admit it."

A High School Leader

Meanwhile, Gertrude had reasons to be proud. The move to Chicago was paying off. John was doing well in school. Even though he spent most of his spare time studying, he still found the time to read Dale Carnegie's famous book *How to Win Friends and Influence People*, a guide to achieving success. With the self-confidence gained from the book, he became business manager of the yearbook, editor-in-chief of the school newspaper, and president of the student council. Finally, he was elected president of his high school.

John Johnson Makes an Impression

At a special assembly for honor students, John met a prominent and important businessman named Harry Pace. Pace, who was also black, was the successful owner of the Supreme Life Insurance Company. He was impressed with the young and ambitious teenager. He asked John what he planned to do with the rest of his life.

John told him that he had received a scholarship to the University of Chicago. He also explained that he couldn't accept the scholarship because he wouldn't have an income to support himself as a full-time

Harry Pace, owner of the Supreme Life Insurance Company, was an early mentor for John. Pace gave John a part-time job so he could afford to attend the University of Chicago.

student. Pace came up with a solution: He would give John a part-time job as an office boy at Supreme Life. With the $25 that he would earn each month, John would be able to begin classes at the University of Chicago.

The teenager could not believe his good fortune. On September 1, 1936, he began life in the business world at Supreme Life. Neither the young office boy nor his bosses realized that one day John Johnson would own the whole company.

3

The Start of Something Big

"All the people who work hard don't succeed, but the <u>only</u> people who succeed are the people who work hard."

Supreme Life was the largest black-owned business in the northern United States. There, John quickly learned about the fine points of running a company tailored for minorities. The men who ran the company experienced prejudice almost daily. Yet, they would not let the ignorance of others prevent the company from succeeding. "I was able to see role models," John said. "I saw well-trained black men who were grappling with the problems of the day, who were making more good decisions than bad, and who were winning more than they were losing."

Climbing the Ladder of Success

John rose up the company's ranks. Because of his background in high school journalism, he was made editor of the company's magazine. Harry Pace, the president and his boss, gave John the task of keeping a collection of articles that were of importance to African Americans. "The president didn't want to read as much as he had before," John explained, "so he gave me a job of reading newspapers and magazines, and giving him a digest of what was happening in the black community each week."

An Idea Is Born

The assortment of articles reminded John of *Reader's Digest*, a popular magazine that took stories from lots of different sources, shortened them, and reprinted them. John came up with an idea: Why not publish a magazine using articles similar to those Pace was receiving? Even though black advances in civil rights were still 20 years off, John knew that changes were coming. African Americans were educating themselves more, but there was no magazine specifically for them. Now, that was going to change—John would create a monthly magazine called *Negro Digest*.

As assistant to Harry Pace, John combed through various magazines and newspapers looking for articles about African Americans.

John had noticed that every minority group that had achieved prosperity so far had begun by focusing on its own needs. Many Italians, for instance, had started in business by selling fruits and vegetables out of pushcarts to other Italians. Jewish Americans had achieved success in the clothing industry after peddling garments in Jewish neighborhoods. John believed that it was important to gain experience by selling to other blacks. Eventually, however, he hoped to expand the business and sell to everyone else.

Bad Advice from Roy Wilkins

Before launching the first issue of *Negro Digest*, John traveled to New York to discuss his plans with Roy Wilkins, editor of *The Crisis*. This was the official magazine of the NAACP (National Association for the Advancement of Colored People), a civil rights group. Surprisingly, Wilkins did not believe that John's *Negro Digest* would sell well. "Save your money, young man," he told John. "Save your energy. Save yourself a lot of disappointment."

Years later, Wilkins—by then a nationally recognized civil rights leader—would admit to Johnson. "You know, I think I gave you some bad advice."

Forging Ahead

John's mother told him to forge ahead with his dream. Blacks in America had long wanted a magazine of their own, she told her son. Now, he would be providing this service for them. She believed that *Negro Digest* would be a winner as long as John was willing to put in the necessary time and a great deal of effort.

"She said that the only people who *do* succeed are the ones who work hard," John recalled. "In other words, all the people who work hard don't succeed, but the *only* people who succeed are the people who work hard. I believed that."

Gertrude even gave her son the money to start the business. She mortgaged her furniture for $500, meaning she agreed to give her household belongings to a bank if *Negro Digest* failed. John used this money to send letters to all of Supreme Life's policyholders. In the letters, he described the magazine and offered a yearly subscription for the rate of $2. About 3,000 readers sent in the money. Now with $6,000 to work with, John was able to print the first issue in November 1942.

Negro Digest Hits the Stands

Getting *Negro Digest* into the magazine stands was another problem. Newsstand owners were not too happy about displaying an African-American publication. John quickly solved this problem. He sent 30 friends to newsstands all over the south side of Chicago, to inquire about *Negro Digest*. Now, the dealers' attitudes changed. They demanded copies of *Negro Digest* for their businesses. John used the same tactic to promote the magazine in New York, Philadelphia, and Detroit.

To make sure local merchants knew people were interested in Negro Digest, John sent 30 friends around to newsstands to ask when the magazine would be available.

The magazine's first headquarters could hardly be called luxurious. John used an empty office in the Supreme Life building. The room was so small that John's first employee had to sit in the hall.

The Right Idea at the Right Time

Despite the early sacrifices, *Negro Digest* seemed to be the right idea at the right time. All 5,000 copies of the first issue sold. Johnson printed 10,000 copies of the second issue. They sold out, too. Month after month, the magazine's readership grew. By its first anniversary, *Negro Digest* had an unbelievable circulation of 50,000!

The success had to do with the fact that blacks were proud of their culture and, according to John, "hungry for information about themselves."

Shortly before he started *Negro Digest*, John had taken a leave of absence from Supreme Life, with the understanding that he could return to work if the magazine failed. Remembering how desperate his parents had been for work after moving to Chicago, John remained on leave of absence for about 20 years—until he finally bought Supreme Life. As he put it, "Never burn your bridges behind you."

Building
an Empire

*"If I can't sell better
than anybody else,
I don't deserve to
be president."*
Three years after the start
of *Negro Digest*, John was ready for his next
big venture—*Ebony*, a magazine filled with
exciting photos and stories focusing on
black history, ambitions, and victories. In
John's mind, African-American culture had
developed since *Negro Digest* began, and the
importance of this type of publication was
never greater.

   "I suppose if *Ebony* didn't exist, some-
body would have to publish it," John later
said. "The need for a magazine that mirrors
the hopes, ideals and accomplishments of
black people throughout the world is just
that great."

Ebony's First Issue

The young publisher went over the first issue carefully. He read the stories again and again, examined the photographs, and made sure the layout (the arrangement of the stories and photos) was pleasing to the eye. He compared himself with a nervous father, who saw his new baby as some part or reflection of himself. His task, he said, was providing "proof to millions of black Americans, young and old, that their dreams can and do come true."

The first issue of *Ebony* was published in November 1945. It contained an assortment of stories about the African-American experience: the appeal of jazz music to both blacks and whites; profiles and interviews with well-known black authors; surveys of African art; an interview with Richard Robert Wright, a 91-year-old former slave who had become a banker.

John printed 25,000 copies of *Ebony*'s first issue. Like *Negro Digest*, circulation grew steadily. Forty years later, 2.3 million copies would be printed each month. Much of the success had to do with the magazine's readers' feeling that *Ebony*—its selection of stories and even its name —was designed specifically for them.

John's wife originally came up with the name *Ebony*. Ebony wood is considered a fine, elegant material. Both the Johnsons wanted readers to view themselves in this same way.

Ebony was the first magazine to use black models in its ads. "We were able to show . . . that if you were appealing to black consumers, an ad with a black model would bring greater results than an ad with a white model," John said. "These things are accepted today, but they were new in the forties. There were no major black models before *Ebony*."

Just as the magazine covered a range of topics, so did its writers. John said, "I want women writing about sports and men about cooking." This widened the reporters' outlooks and formed a reputation for *Ebony* as an open-minded magazine.

His Own Best Salesman

Meanwhile, John came up with creative methods to keep the magazine going. When banks refused to grant him loans, he raised money by selling lifetime subscriptions to *Ebony* for $100 each. To make up for a lack of advertising, he formed a company called Beauty Star. This company sold vitamins, wigs, dresses, and hair-care products by mail. The income from Beauty Star was put back into *Ebony*.

After failing to get a number of big companies to place ads in *Ebony*, John went to see Eugene McDonald, Jr., the president of Zenith. The company was manufacturing radios and would soon be selling televisions. "My mother had a Zenith," John said, "and I knew a lot of black people did."

Eugene McDonald, Jr., president of Zenith, was one of the few people willing to advertise in Ebony. Other companies refused because the magazine was targeted at African-American readers.

Before the 1946 meeting, John carefully researched McDonald's past. He learned that McDonald had taken part in a 1909 expedition to the North Pole under the leadership of Admiral Robert Peary. It just so happened that *Ebony* had recently run a story about Matthew Henson, a black explorer who had been on that same journey. John brought the article to McDonald's office, along with an autographed copy of Henson's autobiography. McDonald pointed to a pair of snow shoes hanging on the wall. "They were given to me by Matthew Henson," he declared. "He is worth any two white men I have ever known."

After further discussion, McDonald looked through a copy of *Ebony* and said, "I don't know why we shouldn't be advertising in this magazine. And you can use my name when you talk to other advertisers."

John continued to take this personal approach to obtain new ads. He actively pursued one company for 20 years before its management decided to place an ad in *Ebony*. Other times, he would drop in on executives who had removed their ads from *Ebony*. He showed them sales figures and persuaded them to advertise in *Ebony* again. "If we lose an account, it's up to me

Despite many obstacles, John continued to push his company forward. During the 1950s, he established *Jet* magazine and the Ebony Fashion Fair.

to get it back," John explained. "If I can't sell better than anybody else, I don't deserve to be president."

Branching Out

As *Ebony*'s popularity swelled, John began enlarging his company. In November of 1951 he started *Jet* magazine. Then, in 1958, he came up with the idea of the

Ebony Fashion Fair, a grand exhibition of

African-American models and designers. Each year, this show travels to over 200 cities and donates $2 million to charity.

Recognizing Women as Equals

Johnson Publishing was obviously different from other large companies because it had black executives. But it also stood apart from other American businesses for another reason—it hired lots of women to fill many of the important positions. John gave his mother all of the credit for having taught him to accept females on equal terms. "I knew that women could achieve," he said. "I knew that women could be relied on and that they could...strive for excellence. I saw the evidence of it in my mother."

The Importance of a Goal

At first, John took pleasure in being wealthy. After the novelty of being rich wore off, he concentrated on the one thing he believed was most important—"the joy of accomplishing a goal."

However, he continued to fly first class, mindful of the condition of blacks forced to "sit in the back of the bus." "We've had second-class treatment long enough," he always said, only half-joking.

5

Covering the Civil Rights Struggle

"The only way he [Martin Luther King, Jr.] got his message across, in the beginning, was through Jet."

Racism was the one topic that haunted the readers of John's publications. While black achievement was always stressed in the magazines, John's employees could not overlook the problems facing African Americans. Johnson himself knew well the pain of prejudice. Once, when he tried to borrow money from a bank, he was dismissed by the bankers, who called him "boy." While traveling the country in search of advertising, he was often turned away from the better hotels.

"We couldn't get a room," John recalled many years later. "So I employed a very light-skinned black man to register for a room at a good hotel. The rest of us went up the freight elevator—everybody assumed we were workmen—and conducted our business in the room without anyone at the hotel knowing we were there."

African Ambassador

As blacks everywhere began to demand their rights, John made certain that *Ebony* and *Jet* thoroughly covered these events. He was often even a part of the news himself.

John served as Special U.S. Ambassador to Ivory Coast during its independence ceremony in 1961. He was accompanied by Robert F. Kennedy.

In 1957, when Africans were calling for freedom from their colonial rulers, John accompanied Vice-President Richard Nixon on a tour of nine African countries. In 1961, President John F. Kennedy sent John as a Special United States Ambassador to Ivory Coast's independence ceremonies. Two years later, President Lyndon Johnson asked him to perform the same task when Kenya's liberty was declared.

Jet Speaks for Martin Luther King, Jr.

But John's greatest concern was always at home, where blacks didn't even have the right to vote in every state until The Voting Rights Act became law in 1965.

On a warm December evening in 1955, a black seamstress named Rosa Parks could not find a seat in the special "Negro section" at the rear of a bus in Montgomery, Alabama. When she sat down in the front and later refused to give up her seat to a white man, she was arrested. The uproar that followed forever changed the way blacks were treated in America.

Martin Luther King, Jr., then a young minister, became the leader of a popular movement against the Montgomery bus service. For 382 days, the city's African

Americans refused to ride the bus. King, aided by civil rights supporters from around the country, organized car pools instead. By the time it all ended, it was obvious that a new day was dawning for blacks.

Johnson Publishing was with King from the start. "When Martin Luther King first began marching," John recalled, "there were no television cameras, there were no white reporters. The only way he got his message across, in the beginning, was through *Jet*."

King's message was one of nonviolence. He insisted that blacks must demand their rights in a dignified fashion, never stooping to brutal methods. "If every Negro in America turns to violence," he once said in *Ebony*, "I'll still stand against it."

Ebony Carries King's Message

In 1963, King was in Birmingham, Alabama, protesting, among other things, the rights of blacks to eat or shop wherever they wished. When he was arrested during the effort, a group of white clergymen asked him to change his methods and wait until the situation improved. From his jail cell in Birmingham, King wrote a famous and dramatic response, which *Ebony* published in its August, 1963 issue.

In 1963, King led 250,000 African-American and white backers of new civil rights laws to Washington, D.C., where he delivered his famous "I Have a Dream" speech. "I have a dream," he pronounced during the historic address, "that one day on the red hills of Georgia, the sons of former slaves and the sons of former slave owners will be able to sit down together at the table of brotherhood."

Ebony called the touching event "the most spectacular nonviolent demonstration this land had ever seen....For one day, it appeared that man might indeed be able to live in peace with his brother."

As demonstrations continued around the country, John's publications did everything possible to ensure that readers understood both sides of the issues. To do this, a black photographer would work with a white photographer. A white journalist would mix with those favoring segregation to get their story. A black reporter would deal with African Americans fighting for the civil rights movement.

On April 4, 1968, King was killed by an assassin while standing on a motel balcony in Memphis, Tennessee. He was in the city to back striking sanitation workers. The

In 1963, Martin Luther King, Jr., delivered his famous "I Have a Dream" speech in Washington, D.C. *Ebony* called it "the most spectacular nonviolent demonstration this land has ever seen."

next month, *Ebony* placed King on its cover and promised that his struggle for understanding between the races would continue.

"Less than 24 hours before his death, King had spelled out the two challenges to America: racism and poverty," *Ebony* reported to its readers. "And he assured all who heard him that he had been to the mountaintop of hope and had seen a Promised Land where such things need not exist." *Ebony* continued to spread King's message.

"His death was not the end of that for which he stood," one article said.

New Opportunities

"I'm in business to make a profit. That's what business means."

"I always say I look for opportunity," John once commented. "I listen for it, and if it knocks on my door, I plan to answer it."

During those times when the doorway was blocked, John found ways to reach it. When he tried to buy his company's first headquarters in Chicago, no one was willing to sell to a black man. John solved the matter by having a white lawyer purchase the facility for him. Later, when he wanted to rent an office in New York's Rockefeller Center, he was told that no space was available. By now, John had a powerful reputation and he used it. He telephoned the building's owner, Winthrop Rockefeller, and asked if anyone was practicing discrimination. Rockefeller made sure that an office was provided to John immediately.

In the 1960s, John sent word throughout Chicago's business community that he was interested in finding a partner to buy a skyscraper with him. Many people called him. But once they realized that he was an African American, however, they changed their minds. "Nobody wanted to go in with me," John said. "I finally had to go it alone by saving money over a long period of time to build a smaller building that only my company could occupy."

A New Home and New Products for Johnson Publications

On December 15, 1971, Johnson Publishing Company opened its new headquarters—the only black-owned and black-constructed office building in Chicago. The structure, with its wide windows and warm colors, was meant to "express the essential meaning of our firm...openness," John said, "openness to truth, openness to light, openness to all the currents swirling in all the black communities of this land."

During the 1970s, John created Ebony Jr!, a children's magazine with puzzles, games, and stories about African-American history.

From his office on Michigan Avenue, in the heart of downtown Chicago, John continued to pursue new ventures. In 1973, after unsuccessfully trying to influence some white-owned cosmetic companies to develop makeup for black consumers, John went ahead and launched Fashion Fair Cosmetics. The Fashion Fair products, specially created for African-American women, would eventually be sold in 2,500 stores in America, Canada, Europe, Africa, and the Caribbean islands.

Ebony Jr!, a children's magazine with puzzles, games, stories about black history, news, and advice, was started the same year.

The End of Negro Digest

Not every moment of John's life has been a triumph. In 1975, he was forced to abandon his original magazine, which had changed its name from *Negro Digest* to *Black World* in 1969. While the other Johnson publications had presented a more positive image of black America, *Black World* was often more critical. When the magazine finally ceased operation, some accused John of trying to portray African Americans in an unrealistic way. But John argued that he had stopped publishing *Black World* because it wasn't making money. "I'm in business to make a profit," he insisted. "That's what business means."

A Son Dies

John's greatest tragedy came in 1981, when his son, John H. Johnson, Jr., died from sickle-cell anemia, an inherited blood disorder that is common to people of West-African descent. John and his wife had adopted the boy as a small child, and they gained great personal satisfaction from caring for their son's special needs. "I couldn't have loved him more, had he been my flesh and blood," John said.

Nursing the youngster through rough periods "was no great burden to me," John emphasized. "It was a joy. I think it was the Lord's will that he be placed in my home so I could prolong his life....He lived to be twenty-five and, I think, given the seriousness of his illness, he probably would have died in his early teens. So I wanted people to know that I never, *never* regretted being his father. I was always proud of it."

Getting Beyond the Sadness

Refusing to allow hardship to set him back, John continued to look forward. In 1983, his company received first place on *Black Enterprise* magazine's list of notable African-American businesses. Johnson Publishing was now the largest black-owned company in the United States.

Two years later, John created *EM*, or *Ebony Man*. Since his other publications had all started in November and had been successful, he published the first issue of *EM* in November 1985.

EM dealt with topics that typically affect the African-American male: careers, fashion,

John has always been active in supporting social causes. Here, he is joined by entertainer Bill Cosby and civil rights activist Jesse Jackson at a charity benefit in 1982.

financial planning, relationships, fatherhood, fitness, and entertainment. "We're looking for young, black, upscale men," John said. "*Ebony Man* is for young black men on the go, young black men who are conscious not only of their grooming and their appearance, but who feel secure about their prospects."

There was also a weekly television show, *Ebony/Jet Showcase*, seen in about 80 cities and towns. A good deal of the show's advertising was for products made by John's other companies. "The more weapons you have to fight with," John said, "the better your chances are of winning the war."

Looking Ahead

"Dream small things because small things can be achieved."

More than 50 years after he started his first magazine, John remains unhappy with the position of blacks in American business. He doesn't think there are enough high-quality black magazines and is upset over the fact that many advertisers have not properly considered the African-American consumer. John is also disappointed that the "best and brightest" in the black community don't seem able to start businesses in their own neighborhoods.

Advice from a Pro

"We have to eat," he said. "Why don't we own our own grocery stores? We eat fried

John remains unhappy about the position of African Americans in business today. Both he and his daughter, Linda, vow to continue to do their share to inspire young African Americans to achieve their goals in America.

chicken. Why don't we own the restaurants? And you know that, in many of the restaurants, the cooks are black. Now, if we know how to cook the food, why can't we sell the food?"

Blacks should realize that many of these small businesses can grow into successful national operations, he insists. "They must understand that a grocery store can indeed develop into a large chain of supermarkets, that a restaurant can indeed become a franchise operation."

His one warning to African-American business owners: "Dream small things, because small things can be achieved. And once you achieve a small dream and make a small success, it gives you the confidence to go on to the next step."

Although John has mainly had African Americans in mind when developing his products, he has often suggested that blacks always look at everyone as a possible client. "If I sold only to black people, I wouldn't have a very successful company," he has said in the past. "Most of my subscriptions and newsstand sales are made to blacks, but ninety percent of my advertising sales are made to whites. So I don't believe that we ought to limit our sales to the black community. I think a black businessman ought to strive to...sell to any customer who will buy from him."

As for blacks already working as executives, his advice is: "Don't sell your abilities short—reach for the top of your profession."

Johnson Publishing—Forever

In an age when many companies encourage senior citizens to resign, John claims he has no desire to slow down. Pointing out that some of Johnson Publishing's most creative and productive workers have been over 65, he said, "As long as I am healthy and active, I will not retire."

But when he does leave the business, and his daughter, Linda, takes over, she won't even think about the idea of selling the company. "Never!" she exclaimed, when asked if she'd ever seek a buyer. "This is Johnson Publishing Company. And I am a Johnson."

Glossary

ambassador Official representative of a country.

assassin Murderer; killer.

circulation Distribution or readership of a magazine or newspaper.

franchise Collection of independently owned businesses each structured on the same model.

layout The visual presentation of a printed piece.

mortgage (verb) To borrow money and offer personal property as insurance against non-payment.

prejudice Discrimination.

racism Prejudice or discrimination based on race.

welfare Financial aid from the government.

For Further Reading

Jacques, Geoffrey. *African-American Movement Today*. New York: Franklin Watts, 1992.

Peters, Margaret W. *Ebony Book of Black Achievement*. Chicago, IL: Johnson Publishing, 1974.

Richardson, Ben, and Foley, William A. *Great Black Americans*. New York: HarperCollins Children's Books, 1990.

Index

Photo Credits:
Cover: ©Jonathan Kirn/Gamma Liaison; p. 4: ©Jonathan
Kirn/Gamma Liaison; p. 8: ©Jonathan Kirn/Gamma
Liaison; p. 28: AP/Wide World Photos; p. 38: Bettmann;
p. 41: AP/Wide World Photos; p. 43: ©C. Johnson/
Gamma Liaison.

Illustrations by Jerry Harston.